MIKE MURDOCK

31

FACTS

· ABOUT ·

WISDOM

Why I Compiled This Book.

Wisdom.

So few ever talk about it.

Everyone shouts Miracles! Love! Healing! Faith! Brotherhood! Family! Salvation!

Yet, *God* said, "Wisdom is the Principal Thing."

So, I decided to discover *why*...Wisdom Is The Most Important Thing In This Life.

Also, I felt that the Family Devotional Times In America are becoming confusing, and quick readings of generic, non-purpose mumblings.

So, I created here a 31 Daily Devotional format to help parents, like myself, who need a Daily Track to keep our kids focused, aware and uncluttered of humanistic poison.

It's simple. Yet, answers every question that really matters in life.

May God bless this Seed into the soil of my generation.

> Pursuing His Wisdom,
> Mike Murdock

---

31 Facts About Wisdom Copyright © 1994 by Mike Murdock
ISBN 1-56394-009-4
Published by Wisdom International • P. O. Box 99 • Denton, Texas 76202

Unless otherwise indicated, all Scripture quotations are taken from the *King James Version* of the Bible.

Printed in the United States of America. All rights reserved under International Copyright Law. Contents and/or cover may not be reproduced in whole or in part in any form without the expressed written consent of the Publisher.

~ 1 ~

WISDOM IS THE MASTER KEY TO ALL THE TREASURES OF LIFE.

"In that night did God appear unto Solomon, and said unto him, Ask what I shall give thee. And Solomon said unto God...Give me now Wisdom and knowledge...And God said to Solomon, Because this was in thine heart, and thou hast not asked riches, wealth, or honour, nor the life of thine enemies, neither yet hast asked long life...Wisdom and knowledge is granted unto thee; and I will give thee riches, and wealth, and honour, such as none of the kings have had that have been before."

2 Chronicles 1:7,8,10,11,12

"In Whom are hid all the treasures of Wisdom and knowledge."

Colossians 2:3

≈ 2 ≈

WISDOM IS A GIFT FROM GOD TO YOU.

"For the Lord *giveth* Wisdom: out of His mouth cometh knowledge and understanding."

Proverbs 2:6

"For to one is *given* by the Spirit the word of Wisdom; to another the word of knowledge by the same Spirit."

1 Corinthians 12:8

"That the God of our Lord Jesus Christ, the Father of glory, may *give* unto you the Spirit of Wisdom and revelation in the knowledge of Him."

Ephesians 1:17

"He *giveth* Wisdom unto the wise, and knowledge to them that know understanding."

Daniel 2:21

☞ 3 ☜

THE FEAR OF GOD IS THE BEGINNING OF WISDOM.

"The fear of the Lord is the beginning of Wisdom: and the knowledge of the holy is understanding."   Proverbs 9:10

"The fear of the Lord is the beginning of Wisdom: a good understanding have all they that do His commandments: His praise endureth forever."
Psalm 111:10

"And unto man he said, Behold, the fear of the Lord, that is Wisdom; and to depart from evil is understanding."   Job 28:28

☞ 4 ☜

THE WISDOM OF MAN IS FOOLISHNESS TO GOD.

"Where is the wise? where is the scribe? where is the disputer of this world? hath not God made foolish the Wisdom of this world? For after that in the Wisdom of God the world by Wisdom knew not God, it pleased God by the foolishness of preaching to save them that believe...Because the foolishness of God is wiser than men; and the weakness of God is stronger than men."   1 Corinthians 1:20,21,25

"For the Wisdom of this world is foolishness with God. For it is written, He taketh the wise in their own craftiness."   1 Corinthians 3:19

∽ 5 ∽

The Wisdom Of This World Is A False Substitute For The Wisdom Of God.

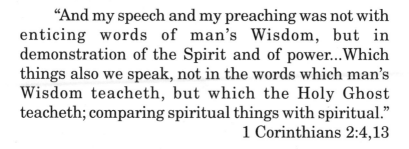

"And my speech and my preaching was not with enticing words of man's Wisdom, but in demonstration of the Spirit and of power...Which things also we speak, not in the words which man's Wisdom teacheth, but which the Holy Ghost teacheth; comparing spiritual things with spiritual."

1 Corinthians 2:4,13

"Who is a wise man and endued with knowledge among you? let him shew out of a good conversation his works with meekness of Wisdom. But if ye have bitter envying and strife in your hearts, glory not, and lie not against the truth. This Wisdom descendeth not from above, but is earthly, sensual, devilish. For where envying and strife is, there is confusion and every evil work. But the Wisdom that is from above is first pure, then peaceable, gentle, and easy to be intreated, full of mercy and good fruits, without partiality, and without hypocrisy."

James 3:13-17

❧ 6 ❧

RELATIONSHIPS INCREASE OR DECREASE YOUR WISDOM.

"He that walketh with wise men shall be wise: but a companion of fools shall be destroyed."

Proverbs 13:20

"Be not deceived: evil communications corrupt good manners."

1 Corinthians 15:33

"Now we command you, brethren, in the name of our Lord Jesus Christ, that ye withdraw yourselves from every brother that walketh disorderly, and not after the tradition which he received of us."

2 Thessalonians 3:6

"Perverse disputings of men of corrupt minds, and destitute of the truth, supposing that gain is godliness: from such withdraw thyself."

1 Timothy 6:5

❧ 7 ❧

THE WISDOM OF GOD IS FOOLISHNESS TO THE NATURAL MIND.

"And my speech and my preaching was not with enticing words of man's Wisdom, but in demonstration of the Spirit and of power: That your faith should not stand in the Wisdom of men, but in the power of God."

1 Corinthians 2:4,5

"A fool hath no delight in understanding."

Proverbs 18:2

"For My thoughts are not your thoughts, neither are your ways My ways, saith the Lord. For as the heavens are higher than the earth, so are My ways higher than your ways, and My thoughts than your thoughts."

Isaiah 55:8,9

⇒ 8 ⇐

Your Conversation Reveals How Much Wisdom You Possess.

⟹ㅡ◉ㅡ⟸

"And all the earth sought to Solomon, to hear his Wisdom, which God had put in his heart."

1 Kings 10:24

"A fool uttereth all his mind: but a wise man keepeth it in till afterwards."

Proverbs 29:11

"Death and life are in the power of the tongue: and they that love it shall eat the fruit thereof."

Proverbs 18:21

"For in many things we offend all. If any man offend not in word, the same is a perfect man, and able also to bridle the whole body."

James 3:2

≈ 9 ≈

JESUS IS MADE UNTO US WISDOM.

"But of Him are ye in Christ Jesus, who of God is made unto us Wisdom, and righteousness, and sanctification, and redemption." 1 Corinthians 1:30

"Having predestinated us unto the adoption of children by Jesus Christ to Himself, according to the good pleasure of His will...Wherein He hath abounded toward us in all Wisdom and prudence... That the God of our Lord Jesus Christ, the Father of glory, may give unto you the spirit of Wisdom and revelation in the knowledge of Him."   Eph. 1:5,8,17

≈ 10 ≈

THE WORD OF GOD IS ABLE TO MAKE YOU WISE CONCERNING SALVATION.

"And that from a child thou hast known the holy Scriptures, which are able to make thee wise unto salvation through faith which is Christ Jesus."
2 Timothy 3:15

"Whoso is wise, and will observe these things, even they shall understand the lovingkindness of the Lord."   Psalm 107:43

"Search the Scriptures; for in them ye think ye have eternal life: and they are they which testify of Me."   John 5:39

≈ 11 ≈

ALL THE TREASURES OF WISDOM AND KNOWLEDGE ARE HID IN JESUS CHRIST.

—————➤●◄—————

"That their hearts might be comforted, being knit together in love, and unto all riches of the full assurance of understanding, to the acknowledgement of the mystery of God, and of the Father, and of Christ: In Whom are hid all the treasures of Wisdom and knowledge."

Colossians 2:2,3

"But we preach Christ crucified, unto the Jews a stumblingblock, and unto the Greeks foolishness; But unto them which are called, both Jews and Greeks, Christ the power of God, and the Wisdom of God."

1 Corinthians 1:23,24

"But we speak the Wisdom of God in a mystery, even the hidden Wisdom, which God ordained before the world unto our glory: Which none of the princes of this world knew: for had they known it, they would not have crucified the Lord of glory."

1 Corinthians 2:7,8

⇜ 12 ⇝

The Word Of God Is
Your Source Of Wisdom.

⇒⊃●⊂⇐

"Behold, I have taught you statutes and judgments, even as the Lord my God commanded me, that ye should do so in the land whither ye go to possess it...For this is your Wisdom and your understanding in the sight of the nations."

Deuteronomy 4:5,6

"Thou through Thy commandments hast made me wiser than mine enemies: for they are ever with me. I have more understanding than all my teachers: for Thy testimonies are my meditation. I understand more than the ancients, because I keep Thy precepts."

Psalm 119:98-100

"For the Lord giveth Wisdom: out of His mouth cometh knowledge and understanding."

Proverbs 2:6

≈ 13 ≈

WISDOM IS ONLY GUARANTEED TO THOSE WHO PURSUE IT.

"For the Lord giveth Wisdom: out of His mouth cometh knowledge and understanding."

Proverbs 2:6

"My sheep hear My voice, and I know them, and they follow Me."

John 10:27

"If any of you lack Wisdom, let him ask of God, that giveth to all men liberally, and upbraideth not; and it shall be given him."

James 1:5

"But they that wait upon the Lord shall renew their strength; they shall mount up with wings as eagles; they shall run, and not be weary; and they shall walk, and not faint."

Isaiah 40:31

≈ 14 ≈

THE HOLY SPIRIT IS THE SPIRIT OF WISDOM THAT UNLEASHES YOUR GIFTS, TALENTS AND SKILLS.

"And the Lord spake unto Moses, saying...And I have filled him with the spirit of God, in Wisdom, and in understanding, and in knowledge, and in all manner of workmanship, To devise cunning works, to work in gold, and in silver, and in brass."

Exodus 31:1,3,4

"In whom the Lord put Wisdom and understanding to know how to work all manner of work for the service of the sanctuary, according to all that the Lord had commanded."

Exodus 36:1

"Children in whom was no blemish, but well favoured, and skilful in all Wisdom, and cunning in knowledge, and understanding science, and such as had ability in them to stand in the king's palace, and whom they might teach the learning and the tongue of the Chaldeans."

Daniel 1:4

∽ 15 ∽

A PERSON OF WISDOM WILL ALWAYS BE A PERSON OF MERCY.

⟩●⟨

"But the Wisdom that is from above is first pure, then peaceable, gentle, and easy to be intreated, full of mercy and good fruits, without partiality, and without hypocrisy."

James 3:17

"Brethren, if any of you do err from the truth, and one convert him; Let him know, that he which converteth the sinner from the error of his way shall save a soul from death, and shall hide a multitude of sins."

James 5:19,20

"Brethren, if a man be overtaken in a fault, ye which are spiritual, restore such an one in the spirit of meekness; considering thyself, lest thou also be tempted. Bear ye one another's burdens, and so fulfill the law of Christ."

Galatians 6:1,2

16

WISDOM IS MORE IMPORTANT THAN JEWELS OR MONEY.

"For Wisdom is better than rubies; and all the things that may be desired are not to be compared to it."

Proverbs 8:11

"Happy is the man that findeth Wisdom, and the man that getteth understanding. For the merchandise of it is better than the merchandise of silver, and the gain thereof than fine gold. She is more precious than rubies; and all the things thou canst desire are not to be compared unto her."

Proverbs 3:13-15

"For the price of Wisdom is above rubies."

Job 28:18

"How much better is it to get Wisdom than gold! and to get understanding rather to be chosen than silver!"

Proverbs 16:16

❧ 17 ❧

WISDOM IS MORE POWERFUL THAN WEAPONS OF WAR.

————⟫●⟪————

"Wisdom is better than weapons of war: but one sinner destroyeth much good."

Ecclesiastes 9:18

"And Wisdom and knowledge shall be the stability of thy times, and strength of salvation: the fear of the Lord is his treasure."

Isaiah 33:6

"But the mouth of the upright shall deliver them."

Proverbs 12:6

"And they were not able to resist the Wisdom and the Spirit by which He spake."

Acts 6:10

≈ 18 ≈

THE MANTLE OF WISDOM MAKES YOU TEN TIMES STRONGER THAN THOSE WITHOUT IT.

⟶➤●ᴳ⟵

"Wisdom strengtheneth the wise more than ten mighty men which are in the city."

Ecclesiastes 7:19

"As for these four children, God gave them knowledge and skill in all learning and Wisdom: and Daniel had understanding in all visions and dreams...And in all matters of Wisdom and understanding, that the king enquired of them, he found them ten times better than all the magicians and astrologers that were in all his realm."

Daniel 1:17,20

"A thousand shall fall at thy side, and ten thousand at thy right hand; but it shall not come nigh thee."

Psalm 91:7

≈ 19 ≈

THE WISE HATE EVIL AND THE EVIL HATE THE WISE.

—————➤●≪—————

"The fear of the Lord is to hate evil: pride, and arrogancy, and the evil way, and the froward mouth, do I hate."

Proverbs 8:13

"The fear of the Lord is the beginning of knowledge: but fools despise Wisdom and instruction."

Proverbs 1:7

"Reprove not a scorner, lest he hate thee: rebuke a wise man, and he will love thee."

Proverbs 9:8

"A fool hath no delight in understanding."

Proverbs 18:2

"How long, ye simple ones, will ye love simplicity? and the scorners delight in their scorning, and fools hate knowledge?"

Proverbs 1:22

❧ 20 ❧

WISDOM CAN REVEAL THE TREASURE HIDDEN WITHIN YOU.

━━━━━━━❯━●━❮━━━━━

"He that getteth Wisdom loveth his own soul: he that keepeth understanding shall find good."

Proverbs 19:8

"That the communication of thy faith may become effectual by the acknowledging of every good thing which is in you in Christ Jesus."

Philemon 6

"But ye are a chosen generation, a royal priesthood, an holy nation, a peculiar people; that ye should shew forth the praises of Him who hath called you out of darkness into His marvellous light: Which in time past were not a people, but are now the people of God: which had not obtained mercy, but now have obtained mercy."

1 Peter 2:9,10

"For we are His workmanship, created in Christ Jesus unto good works, which God hath before ordained that we should walk in them."

Ephesians 2:10

✧ 21 ✧

THE PROOF OF WISDOM IS THE PRESENCE OF JOY AND PEACE.

"For Wisdom is a defence, and money is a defence: but the excellency of knowledge is, that Wisdom giveth life to them that have it."

Ecclesiastes 7:12

"Happy is the man that findeth Wisdom, and the man that getteth understanding."

Proverbs 3:13

"But the Wisdom that is from above is first pure, then peaceable, gentle, and easy to be intreated, full of mercy and good fruits, without partiality, and without hypocrisy."

James 3:17

"Great peace have they which love Thy law: and nothing shall offend them."

Psalm 119:165

22

Wisdom Makes Your Enemies Helpless Against You.

"For I will give you a mouth and Wisdom, which all your adversaries shall not be able to gainsay nor resist."

Luke 21:15

"When a man's ways please the Lord, He maketh even his enemies to be at peace with him."

Proverbs 16:7

"No weapon that is formed against thee shall prosper; and every tongue that shall rise against thee in judgment thou shalt condemn. This is the heritage of the servants of the Lord, and their righteousness is of Me, saith the Lord."

Isaiah 54:17

"For Wisdom is a defence, and money is a defence."

Ecclesiastes 7:12

"For the Lord giveth Wisdom...To deliver thee from the way of the evil man...To deliver thee from the strange woman."

Proverbs 2:6,12,16

≈ 23 ≈

WISDOM CREATES CURRENTS OF FAVOR TOWARD YOU.

"Exalt her, and she shall promote thee: she shall bring thee to honour, when thou dost embrace her."
Proverbs 4:8

"Blessed is the man that heareth Me, watching daily at My gates, waiting at the posts of My doors. For whoso findeth Me findeth life, and shall obtain favour of the Lord."
Proverbs 8:34,35

"My son, forget not My law...So shalt thou find favour and good understanding in the sight of God and man."
Proverbs 3:1,4

≋ 24 ≋

THE WISE WELCOME CORRECTION.

"Reprove not a scorner, lest he hate thee: rebuke a wise man, and he will love thee. Give instruction to a wise man, and he will be yet wiser: teach a just man, and he will increase in learning."   Prov. 9:8,9

"The ear that heareth the reproof of life abideth among the wise. He that refuseth instruction despiseth his own soul: but he that heareth reproof getteth understanding."   Proverbs 15:31,32

"My son, despise not the chastening of the Lord; neither be weary of His correction: For whom the Lord loveth He correcteth; even as a father the son in whom he delighteth."   Proverbs 3:11,12

≋ 25 ≋

WISDOM LOVES THOSE WHO LOVE HER.

"I love them that love Me; and those that seek Me early shall find Me."   Proverbs 8:17

"That I may cause those that love Me to inherit substance; and I will fill their treasures." Prov. 8:21

"Yea, if thou criest after knowledge, and liftest up thy voice for understanding; If thou seekest her as silver, and searchest for her as for hid treasures; Then shalt thou understand the fear of the Lord, and find the knowledge of God."   Proverbs 2:3-5

~ 26 ~

WHEN YOU INCREASE YOUR WISDOM YOU WILL INCREASE YOUR WEALTH.

"Riches and honour are with me; yea, durable riches and righteousness...That I may cause those that love me to inherit substance; and I will fill their treasures."

Proverbs 8:18,21

"Length of days is in her right hand; and in her left hand riches and honour."

Proverbs 3:16

"Blessed is the man that feareth the Lord, that delighteth greatly in His commandments...Wealth and riches shall be in his house."

Psalm 112:1,3

"The crown of the wise is their riches."

Proverbs 14:24

✑ 27 ✑

WISDOM CAN BE IMPARTED BY THE LAYING ON OF HANDS BY A MAN OF GOD.

"And Joshua the son of Nun was full of the Spirit of Wisdom; for Moses had laid his hands upon him: and the children of Israel hearkened unto him, and did as the Lord commanded Moses."

Deuteronomy 34:9

"Wherefore I put thee in remembrance that thou stir up the gift of God, which is in thee by the putting on of my hands...That good thing which was committed unto thee keep by the Holy Ghost which dwelleth in us."

2 Timothy 1:6,14

"Whom they set before the apostles: and when they had prayed, they laid their hands on them. And Stephen, full of faith and power, did great wonders and miracles among the people. And they were not able to resist the Wisdom and the Spirit by which he spake."

Acts 6:6,8,10

≈ 28 ≈

WISDOM GUARANTEES PROMOTION.

————◄►————

"By me kings reign, and princes decree justice. By me princes rule, and nobles, even all the judges of the earth."

Proverbs 8:15,16

"And thou, Ezra, after the Wisdom of thy God, that is in thine hand, set magistrates and judges, which may judge all the people that are beyond the river, all such as know the laws of thy God; and teach ye them that know them not."

Ezra 7:25

"Exalt her, and she shall promote thee: she shall bring thee to honour, when thou dost embrace her. She shall give to thine head an ornament of grace: a crown of glory shall she deliver to thee."

Proverbs 4:8,9

～ 29 ～

WHEN THE WISE SPEAK, HEALING FLOWS.

"There is that speaketh like the piercings of a sword: but the tongue of the wise is health."

Proverbs 12:18

"The tongue of the wise useth knowledge aright: but the mouth of fools poureth out foolishness...A wholesome tongue is a tree of life: but perverseness therein is a breach in the spirit."

Proverbs 15:2,4

"The tongue of the just is as choice silver...The lips of the righteous feed many."

Proverbs 10:20,21

"Death and life are in the power of the tongue: and they that love it shall eat the fruit thereof."

Proverbs 18:21

"The mouth of a righteous man is a well of life: but violence covereth the mouth of the wicked."

Proverbs 10:11

≈ 30 ≈

WISDOM WILL BE GIVEN TO YOU WHEN YOU ASK FOR IT IN FAITH.

"If any of you lack Wisdom, let him ask of God, that giveth to all men liberally, and upbraideth not; and it shall be given him. But let him ask in faith, nothing wavering."

James 1:5,6

"Ask, and it shall be given you; seek, and ye shall find; knock, and it shall be opened unto you: For every one that asketh receiveth; and he that seeketh findeth; and to him that knocketh it shall be opened...If ye then, being evil, know how to give good gifts unto your children, how much more shall your Father which is in heaven give good things to them that ask Him?"

Matthew 7:7,8,11

~ 31 ~

HE THAT WINS SOULS IS WISE.

⟶►●◄⟵

"The fruit of the righteous is a tree of life; and he that winneth souls is wise."

Proverbs 11:30

"And they that be wise shall shine as the brightness of the firmament; and they that turn many to righteousness as the stars for ever and ever."

Daniel 12:3

"How then shall they call on Him in whom they have not believed? and how shall they believe in Him of whom they have not heard? and how shall they hear without a preacher? And how shall they preach, except they be sent? as it is written, How beautiful are the feet of them that preach the gospel of peace, and bring glad tidings of good things!"

Romans 10:14,15

DECISION

Will You Accept Jesus As Your Personal Savior Today?

The Bible says, "That if thou shalt confess with thy mouth the Lord Jesus, and shalt believe in thine heart that God hath raised Him from the dead, thou shalt be saved" (Rom. 10:9).

Pray this prayer from your heart today!

"Dear Jesus, I believe that You died for me and rose again on the third day. I confess I am a sinner...I need Your love and forgiveness... Come into my heart. Forgive my sins. I receive your eternal life. Confirm Your love by giving me peace, joy and supernatural love for others. Amen."

DR. MIKE MURDOCK

is in tremendous demand as one of the most dynamic speakers in America today.

More than 14,000 audiences in 38 countries have attended his meetings and seminars. Hundreds of invitations come to him from churches, colleges and business corporations. He is a noted author of over 120 books, including the best sellers, *"The Leadership Secrets of Jesus"* and *"Secrets of the Richest Man Who Ever Lived."* Thousands view his weekly television program, *"Wisdom Keys with Mike Murdock."* Many attend his Saturday School of Wisdom Breakfasts that he hosts in major cities of America.

Clip and Mail

❑ Yes, Mike! I made a decision to accept Christ as my personal Savior today. Please send me my free gift of your book, *"31 Keys to a New Beginning"* to help me with my new life in Christ. *(B48)*

NAME _____ BIRTHDAY _____

ADDRESS _____

CITY _____ STATE _____ ZIP _____

PHONE _____ E-MAIL _____ *B46*

Mail form to:

The Wisdom Center • P. O. Box 99 • Denton, TX 76202
Phone: 940-891-1400 • Fax: 940-891-4500
Website: www.thewisdomcenter.cc

Your Letter Is Very Important To Me

. . . .

Y ou are a special person to me, and I believe that you are special to God. I want to assist you in any way possible. Write me when you need an intercessor to pray for you. When you write, my staff and I will pray over your letter. I will write you back to help you receive the miracle you need.

Mike, please enter into the prayer of agreement with me for the following needs:

(Please Print)

_____

_____

_____

_____

_____

_____

_____

_____

_____

Mail to:
DR. MIKE MURDOCK
P. O. Box 99
Denton, Texas 76202
(940) 891-1400 • Fax: (940) 891-4500
Website: **www.thewisdomcenter.cc**

· Clip and Mail ·

WISDOM 12 PAK

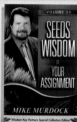

THE MASTER SECRET OF LIFE IS WISDOM
Ignorance Is The Only True Enemy Capable Of Destroying You (Hosea 4:6, Proverbs 11:14)

▶ 1.	MY PERSONAL DREAM BOOK	B143	$5.00
▶ 2.	THE COVENANT OF FIFTY-EIGHT BLESSINGS	B47	$8.00
▶ 3.	WISDOM, GOD'S GOLDEN KEY TO SUCCESS	B71	$7.00
▶ 4.	SEEDS OF WISDOM ON THE HOLY SPIRIT	B116	$5.00
▶ 5.	SEEDS OF WISDOM ON THE SECRET PLACE	B115	$5.00
▶ 6.	SEEDS OF WISDOM ON THE WORD OF GOD	B117	$5.00
▶ 7.	SEEDS OF WISDOM ON YOUR ASSIGNMENT	B122	$5.00
▶ 8.	SEEDS OF WISDOM ON PROBLEM SOLVING	B118	$5.00
▶ 9.	101 WISDOM KEYS	B45	$7.00
▶ 10.	31 KEYS TO A NEW BEGINNING	B48	$7.00
▶ 11.	THE PROVERBS 31 WOMAN	B49	$7.00
▶ 12.	31 FACTS ABOUT WISDOM	B46	$7.00

Wisdom Is The Principal Thing

Book Pak
WBL-12 / $30
(A $73 Value!)

The Wisdom Center

ORDER TODAY!
www.thewisdomcenter.cc

1-888-WISDOM-1
(1-888-947-3661)

THE WISDOM CENTER • P.O. Box 99 • Denton, Texas 76202

33

Money Matters:

This Powerful Video will unleash the Financial Harvest of your lifetime!

VIDEO

31 REAON
PEOPLE DO NOT RECEIVE THEIR
FINANCIAL HARVE$T

MIKE MURDOCK

▶ 8 Scriptural Reasons You Should Pursue Financial Prosperity

▶ The Secret Prayer Key You Need When Making A Financial Request To God

▶ The Weapon Of Expectation And The 5 Miracles It Unlocks

▶ How To Discern Those Who Qualify To Receive Your Financial Assistance

▶ How To Predict The Miracle Moment God Will Schedule Your Financial Breakthrough

Wisdom Is The Principal Thing

Video VI-17 / **$30**

Six Audio Tapes / **$30** TS-71

Book / **$12** B-82

The Wisdom Center

THE WISDOM CENTER

ORDER TODAY!
www.thewisdomcenter.cc

1-888-WISDOM-1
(1-888-947-3661)

THE WISDOM CENTER • P.O. Box 99 • Denton, Texas 76202

34

The Secret To 1000 Times More.

In this Dynamic Video you will find answers to unleash Financial Flow into your life!

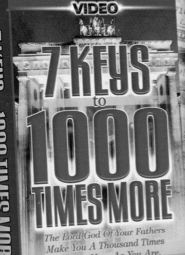

7 KEYS to 1000 TIMES MORE

VIDEO

7 KEYS to 1000 TIMES MORE

The Lord God Of Your Fathers Make You A Thousand Times So Many More As You Are, And Bless You, As He Hath Promised You!
Deuteronomy 1:11

MIKE MURDOCK

▶ **Habits Of Uncommon Achievers**

▶ **The Greatest Success Law I Ever Discovered**

▶ **How To Discern Your Place Of Assignment, The Only Place Financial Provision Is Guaranteed**

▶ **3 Secret Keys In Solving Problems For Others**

▶ **How To Become The Next Person To Receive A Raise On Your Job**

Wisdom Is The Principal Thing

Video VI-16 / **$30**

Six Audio Tapes / **$30** TS-104

Book / **$10** B-104

The Wisdom Center

THE WISDOM CENTER

ORDER TODAY!
www.thewisdomcenter.cc

1-888-WISDOM-1
(1-888-947-3661)

THE WISDOM CENTER • P.O. Box 99 • Denton, Texas 76202

Somebody's Future
Will Not Begin Until You Enter.

THIS COLLECTION INCLUDES 4 DIFFERENT BOOKS CONTAINING UNCOMMON WISDOM FOR DISCOVERING YOUR LIFE ASSIGNMENT

▸ How To Achieve A God-Given Dream And Goal

▸ How To Know Who Is Assigned To You

▸ The Purpose And Rewards Of An Enemy

Wisdom Is The Principal Thing
Book Pak
WBL-14 / **$30**
Buy 3-Get 1 Free
($10 Each/$40 Value!)
The Wisdom Center

ORDER TODAY!
www.thewisdomcenter.cc

1-888-WISDOM-1
(1-888-947-3661)

THE WISDOM CENTER • P.O. Box 99 • Denton, Texas 76202

The Secret Place

Library Pak

Songs From The Secret Place

Over 40 Great Songs On 6 Music Tapes
Including "I'm In Love" / Love Songs From The Holy Spirit
Birthed In The Secret Place / Side A Is Dr. Mike Murdock
Singing / Side B Is Music Only For Your Personal Prayer Time

Seeds Of Wisdom On The Secret Place

4 Secrets The Holy Spirit Reveals In The Secret Place /
The Necessary Ingredients In Creating Your Secret Place /
10 Miracles That Will Happen In The Secret Place

Wisdom Is The Principal Thing

Book/Tape Pak
SP PAK-001 / $30
Six Audio Tapes & Two Books
(A $40 Value!)

The Wisdom Center

Seeds Of Wisdom On The Holy Spirit

The Protocol For Entering The Presence Of The Holy Spirit /
The Greatest Day Of My Life And What Made It So /
Power Keys For Developing Your Personal Relationship With The Holy Spirit

Getting Past The Pain.

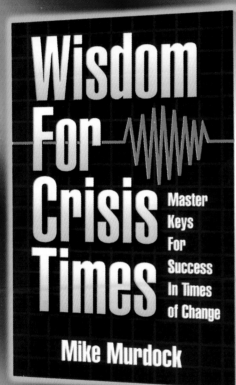

- ▶ **6 Essential Facts That Must Be Faced When Recovering From Divorce**

- ▶ **4 Forces That Guarantee Career Success**

- ▶ **3 Ways Crisis Can Help You**

- ▶ **4 Reasons You Are Experiencing Opposition To Your Assignment**

- ▶ **How To Predict The 6 Seasons Of Attack On Your Life**

- ▶ **4 Keys That Can Shorten Your Present Season Of Struggle**

- ▶ **2 Important Facts You Must Know About Battle & Warfare**

- ▶ **6 Weapons Satan Uses To Attack Marriages**

Wisdom For Crisis Times will give you the answers to the struggle you are facing now, and any struggle you could ever face. Dr. Murdock presents practical steps to help you walk through your "Seasons of Fire."

Wisdom Is The Principal Thing
Book B-40 / **$9**
Six Audio Tapes TS-69 / **$30**
The Wisdom Center

- ▶ **96 Wisdom Keys from God's Word** will direct you into the success that God intended for your life. This teaching will unlock the door to your personal happiness, peace of mind, fulfillment and success.

THE WISDOM CENTER

ORDER TODAY!
www.thewisdomcenter.cc

1-888-WISDOM-1
(1-888-947-3661)

THE WISDOM CENTER • P.O. Box 99 • Denton, Texas 76202

The SCHOOL of WISDOM

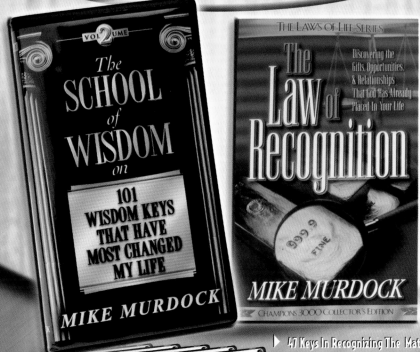

VOLUME 2

The SCHOOL of WISDOM on

101 WISDOM KEYS THAT HAVE MOST CHANGED MY LIFE

MIKE MURDOCK

THE LAWS OF LIFE SERIES

The Law of Recognition

Discovering the Gifts, Opportunities, & Relationships That God Has Already Placed In Your Life

MIKE MURDOCK

CHAMPIONS 3000 COLLECTOR'S EDITION

DR. MIKE MURDOCK
P.O. BOX 99 • DALLAS, TEXAS • 75221

The School of Wisdom

▸ 47 Keys In Recognizing The Mate God Has Approved For You

▸ 14 Facts You Should Know About Your Gifts and Talents

▸ 17 Important Facts You Should Remember About Your Weakness

▸ And Much, Much More...

▸ What Attracts Others Toward You

▸ The Secret Of Multiplying Your Financial Blessings

▸ What Stops The Flow Of Your Faith

▸ Why Some Fail And Others Succeed

▸ How To Discern Your Life Assignment

▸ How To Create Currents Of Favor With Others

▸ How To Defeat Loneliness

Wisdom Is The Principal Thing

Book/Tape Pak
PAK-002 / **$30**
Six Audio Tapes & Book
(A $40 Value!)

The Wisdom Center

THE WISDOM CENTER

ORDER TODAY!
www.thewisdomcenter.cc

1-888-WISDOM-1
(1-888-947-3661)

THE WISDOM CENTER • P.O. Box 99 • Denton, Texas 76202

Learn From The Greatest.

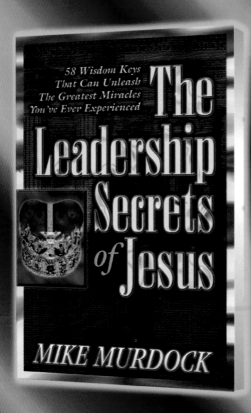

- ▸ The Secret Of Handling Rejection
- ▸ How To Deal With The Mistakes Of Others
- ▸ 5 Power Keys For Effective Delegation To Others
- ▸ The Key To Developing Great Faith
- ▸ The Greatest Qualities Of Champions
- ▸ The Secret Of The Wealthy
- ▸ 4 Goal-Setting Techniques
- ▸ 10 Facts Jesus Taught About Money

In this dynamic and practical guidebook Mike Murdock points you directly to Jesus, the Ultimate Mentor. You'll take just a moment every day to reflect on His life and actions. And when you do, you'll discover all the key skills and traits that Jesus used... the powerful "leadership secrets" that build true, lasting achievement. Explore them. Study them. Put them to work in your own life and your success will be assured!

Wisdom Is The Principal Thing

Book B-91 / $10

The Wisdom Center

THE WISDOM CENTER

ORDER TODAY!
www.thewisdomcenter.cc

1-888-WISDOM-1
(1-888-947-3661)

THE WISDOM CENTER • P.O. Box 99 • Denton, Texas 76202

Your Rewards In Life Are Determined By The Problems You Solve.

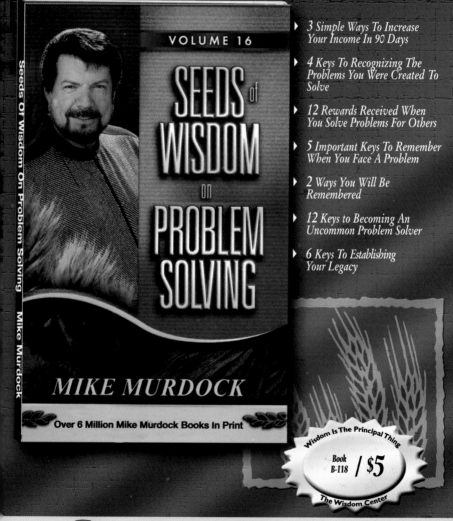

VOLUME 16

SEEDS of WISDOM on PROBLEM SOLVING

MIKE MURDOCK

Over 6 Million Mike Murdock Books In Print

Seeds Of Wisdom On Problem Solving — Mike Murdock

▸ *3 Simple Ways To Increase Your Income In 90 Days*

▸ *4 Keys To Recognizing The Problems You Were Created To Solve*

▸ *12 Rewards Received When You Solve Problems For Others*

▸ *5 Important Keys To Remember When You Face A Problem*

▸ *2 Ways You Will Be Remembered*

▸ *12 Keys to Becoming An Uncommon Problem Solver*

▸ *6 Keys To Establishing Your Legacy*

Wisdom Is The Principal Thing

Book B-118 / $5

The Wisdom Center

THE WISDOM CENTER

ORDER TODAY!
www.thewisdomcenter.cc

1-888-WISDOM-1
(1-888-947-3661)

THE WISDOM CENTER • P.O. Box 99 • Denton, Texas 76202

You Can Have It.

- ▸ **Why Sickness Is Not The Will Of God**
- ▸ **How To Release The Powerful Forces That Guarantee Blessing**
- ▸ **The Incredible Role Of Your Memory And The Imagination**
- ▸ **The Hidden Power Of Imagination And How To Use It Properly**
- ▸ **The Difference Between The Love Of God And His Blessings**
- ▸ **3 Steps In Increasing Your Faith**
- ▸ **2 Rewards That Come When You Use Your Faith In God**
- ▸ **7 Powerful Keys Concerning Your Faith**

Dreams and desires begin as photographs within our hearts and minds - things that we want to happen in our future. God plants these pictures as invisible Seeds within us. God begins every miracle in your life with a Seed-picture... the invisible idea that gives birth to a visible blessing. In this teaching, you will discover your desires and how to concentrate on watering and nurturing the growth of your Dream-Seeds until you attain your God-given goals.

Wisdom Is The Principal Thing

Book B-11 / **$9**

Six Audio Tapes TS-2 / **$30**

The Wisdom Center

THE WISDOM CENTER

42

ORDER TODAY!
www.thewisdomcenter.cc

1-888-WISDOM-1
(1-888-947-3661)

THE WISDOM CENTER • P.O. Box 99 • Denton, Texas 76202

Where You Are Determines What Grows In You.

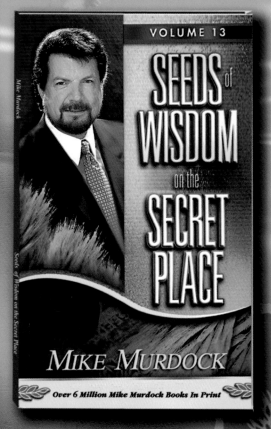

VOLUME 13

SEEDS of WISDOM on the SECRET PLACE

MIKE MURDOCK

Over 6 Million Mike Murdock Books In Print

▶ 4 Secrets The Holy Spirit Reveals In The Secret Place

▶ Master Keys In Cultivating An Effective Prayer Life

▶ The Necessary Ingredients In Creating Your Secret Place

▶ 10 Miracles That Will Happen In The Secret Place

Wisdom Is The Principal Thing

Book B-115 / $5

The Wisdom Center

THE WISDOM CENTER

ORDER TODAY!
www.thewisdomcenter.cc

**1-888-WISDOM-1
(1-888-947-3661)**

THE WISDOM CENTER • P.O. Box 99 • Denton, Texas 76202

Run To Win.

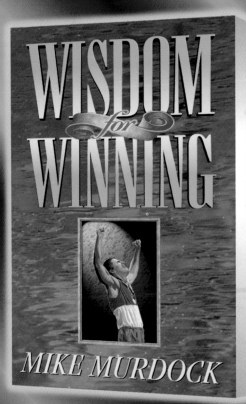

- ▸ 10 Ingredients For Success
- ▸ 10 Lies Many People Believe About Money
- ▸ 20 Keys For Winning At Work
- ▸ 20 Keys To A Better Marriage
- ▸ 3 Facts Every Parent Should Remember
- ▸ 5 Steps Out Of Depression
- ▸ The Greatest Wisdom Principle I Ever Learned
- ▸ 7 Keys To Answered Prayer
- ▸ God's Master Golden Key To Total Success
- ▸ The Key To Understanding Life

Everyone needs to feel they have achieved something with their life. When we stop producing, loneliness and laziness will choke all enthusiasm from our living. What would you like to be doing? What are you doing about it? Get started on a project in your life. Start building on your dreams. Resist those who would control and change your personal goals. Get going with this powerful teaching and reach your life goals!

Wisdom Is The Principal Thing

Book B-01 / **$10**

Six Audio Tapes TS-01 / **$30**

The Wisdom Center

THE WISDOM CENTER

ORDER TODAY!
www.thewisdomcenter.cc

1-888-WISDOM-1
(1-888-947-3661)

THE WISDOM CENTER • P.O. Box 99 • Denton, Texas 76202

THE SECRET.

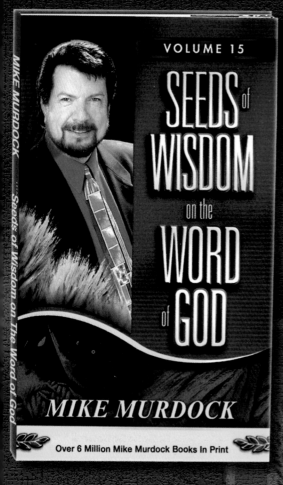

VOLUME 15

SEEDS of WISDOM on the WORD of GOD

MIKE MURDOCK

Over 6 Million Mike Murdock Books In Print

- ▸ 11 Reasons Why The Bible Is The Most Important Book On Earth

- ▸ 12 Problems The Word Of God Can Solve In Your Life

- ▸ 4 Of My Personal Bible Reading Secrets

- ▸ 4 Steps To Building A Spiritual Home

- ▸ 9 Wisdom Keys To Being Successful In Developing The Habit Of Reading The Word Of God

Wisdom Is The Principal Thing

Book B-117 / $5

The Wisdom Center

THE WISDOM CENTER

ORDER TODAY!
www.thewisdomcenter.cc

1-888-WISDOM-1
(1-888-947-3661)

THE WISDOM CENTER • P.O. Box 99 • Denton, Texas 76202

Your Assignment Is Your Discovery, Not Your Decision.

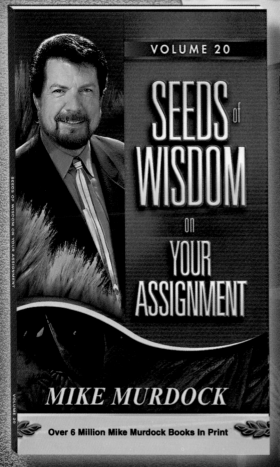

VOLUME 20

SEEDS of WISDOM on YOUR ASSIGNMENT

MIKE MURDOCK

Over 6 Million Mike Murdock Books In Print

- ▶ 11 Seasons Of Preparation For Your Assignment

- ▶ 6 Rewards Of Pain

- ▶ 6 Keys For Developing An Obsession For Your Assignment

- ▶ 3 Wisdom Keys To Turning Your Anger Into Passion For Your Assignment

Wisdom Is The Principal Thing

Book B-122 / **$5**

The Wisdom Center

THE WISDOM CENTER

46

ORDER TODAY!
www.thewisdomcenter.cc

1-888-WISDOM-1
(1-888-947-3661)

THE WISDOM CENTER • P.O. Box 99 • Denton, Texas 76202

WISDOM COLLECTION

8

SECRETS OF THE UNCOMMON MILLIONAIRE

1. The Uncommon Millionaire Conference Vol. 1 (Six Cassettes)
2. The Uncommon Millionaire Conference Vol. 2 (Six Cassettes)
3. The Uncommon Millionaire Conference Vol. 3 (Six Cassettes)
4. The Uncommon Millionaire Conference Vol. 4 (Six Cassettes)
5. 31 Reasons People Do Not Receive Their Financial Harvest (256 Page Book)
6. Secrets Of the Richest Man Who Ever Lived (178 Page Book)
7. 12 Seeds Of Wisdom Books On 12 Topics
8. The Gift Of Wisdom For Leaders Desk Calendar
9. 101 Wisdom Keys On Tape (Audio Tape)
10. In Honor Of The Holy Spirit (Music Cassette)
11. 365 Memorization Scriptures On The Word Of God (Audio Cassette)

Wisdom Is The Principal Thing
THE WISDOM COLLECTION 8
SECRETS OF THE UNCOMMON
MILLIONAIRE
WC-08 /$195
The Wisdom Center

The WISDOM CENTER

ORDER TODAY!
www.thewisdomcenter.cc

1-888-WISDOM-1
(1-888-947-3661)

THE WISDOM CENTER • P.O. Box 99 • Denton, Texas 76202

The Secrets For Surviving.

How To Get Through The Storms Of Your Life!

Avoiding the #1 Trap Satan Uses Against Believers!

Keys To Discovering Wrong People In Your Life!

Satan's 3 Most Effective Weapons!

How To Use Adversity As A Stepping Stone To Wisdom!

How To Stand When Everything Is Falling Apart!

7 Seasons Satan Always Attacks You!

Battle Techniques Of War-Weary Saints!

Reversing Satanic Strategy!

How To Get Back Up When The Devil Puts You Down!

A DOUBLE DIAMOND COLLECTION

The Double Diamond
AND
SURVIVING THE STORMS

- How to Get Through the Storms of Life
- Satan's Most Effective Weapons
- How to Stand When Everything is Falling Apart
- Battle Techniques for War-Weary Saints
- How to Get Back Up When the Devil Puts You Down
- Reversing Satanic Strategy

Dr. Mike Murdock

TS 18

DR. MIKE MURDOCK
Surviving The Storms

Six Wisdom Cassettes That Will Multiply Your Success!

This life changing and revolutionary teaching is based on the Wisdom and The Principles of other champions in the Word of God. You will discover the greatest Wisdom Keys on earth and will begin unlocking the treasure containing every desired gift and miracle you are pursuing.

Wisdom Is The Principal Thing
Tape Pak TS-18 / $30
Six Audio Tapes
The Wisdom Center

ORDER TODAY!
www.thewisdomcenter.cc

1-888-WISDOM-1
(1-888-947-3661)

THE WISDOM CENTER • P.O. Box 99 • Denton, Texas 76202

48